KETOGENIC

DIET

60 MOUTHWATERING MEALS

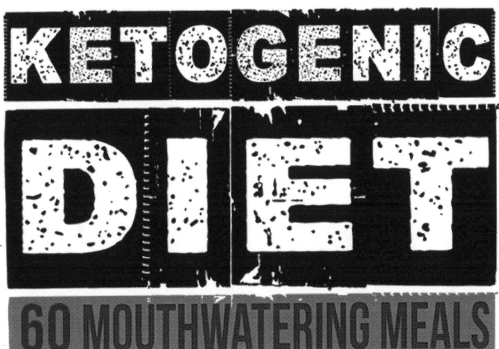

KETOGENIC DIET

60 MOUTHWATERING MEALS

1 MONTH OF LOW-CARB, HIGH-FAT WEIGHT LOSS MEALS

Recipes365

• BEFORE YOU BEGIN •

Free Bonus Guide:

Top 10 Ketogenic Diet Mistakes

We've put together a free companion guide to go with this recipe book. It features the top 10 mistakes made by people on the ketogenic diet.

If you want to avoid costly mistakes and accelerate your progress you will find a link below to get it below now!

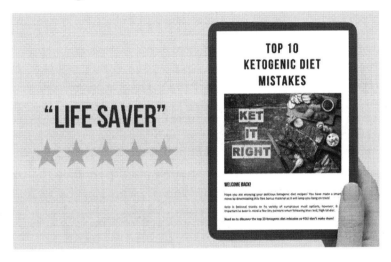

Visit www.litomedia.com/ketogenic-mistakes to get your free bonus guide!

Table of Contents

Lunches

Dinners

"One cannot think well, love well, sleep well, if one has not dined well."

-Virginia Woolf

INTRODUCTION

Welcome to the world's most effective high-fat, low-carb diet! By now you are probably well aware of the benefits of going keto, but just in case you need to refresh your memory here's a quick top-up before we dive into the recipes.

THE SCIENCE IN A NUTSHELL

Your body normally converts carbohydrates into glucose for energy. By limiting your intake and replacing it with fats, your body enters a state of ketosis.

Here your body produces ketones, created by a breakdown of fats in the liver. Without carbohydrates as your primary source of energy your body will turn to the ketones instead.

This effectively cranks up the fat burning furnace and puts your body in the ultimate metabolic state.

WHAT KETO CAN DO FOR YOU

Keto has its origins in treating healthcare conditions such as epilepsy, diabetes, cardiovascular disease, metabolic syndrome, auto-brewery syndrome and high blood pressure but now has much wider application in weight control.

This diet, then, will take you above and beyond typical results and propel you into a new realm of total body health. If you want to look and feel the best you possibly can, all without sacrificing your love of delicious food, then this is the cookbook for you.

THINGS TO REMEMBER

A good diet is not solution to anything in and of itself; it must be applied as part of a healthy lifestyle in order to see maximum results.

Think of the ketogenic diet as the foundation for your new body. If you want to build something truly special on top of it then design your lifestyle with that goal in mind.

Cutting out junk food goes without saying, as does ditching bad habits such as smoking and drinking. Exercise, too, will take you to heights you never knew were possible.

So, as you explore these delectable dishes and embark on the keto diet, try not to neglect other areas or responsibility.

We recommend getting some professional advice from a physician prior to commencing, since they will be able to advise you much better on your own individual goals.

With that said, we just know you will love every bite of what's to come. Don't forget to share the love and tell a friend. Having them with you on this journey will be incredibly motivational.

This is the start of something great. Let's go!

THE RECIPES

We wanted to make it as simple as possible for you to get in the kitchen and rustle up something special, so you will find each recipe laid out in an easy to follow format.

Each begins with a short intro to the dish, followed by the serving size and list of ingredients. Remember, this diet is designed to rekindle your love of food, not extinguish it with rules and regulations, so don't be afraid to experiment.

Use the ingredients as general guidelines and follow the instructions as best you can. You may not get everything perfect first time, every time, but that is what makes it yours!

Cooking and eating shouldn't be about presentation, so you won't find any fancy pictures here. In fact, you won't find any pictures at all, because they will just distract you from your goals.

When you obsess over replicating recipes to the exact photographic standards of a professional chef it becomes an impossible task. Instead, simply follow the recipes and find your own rhythm. Soon enough, you'll have created your own signature dishes!

Each recipe ends with a breakdown of key nutritional information including number of calories and amount of fats, carbohydrates and protein.

Again, this isn't to be obsessed over. Food is something to be enjoyed, so don't go trying to calculate your macros to four decimal points! Be responsible when monitoring your progress, but be reasonable, too.

Once you start loving what you are eating mealtimes will become something to look forward to, and that's when the magic happens.

So without further ado, go forth, and cook to your heart's content!

"Eating is not merely a material pleasure. Eating well gives a spectacular joy to life and contributes immensely to goodwill and happy companionship. It is of great importance to the morale."

-Elsa Schiaparelli

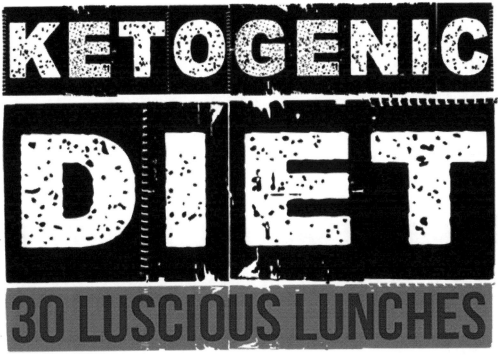

KETOGENIC DIET

30 LUSCIOUS LUNCHES

1 MONTH OF LOW-CARB, HIGH-FAT WEIGHT LOSS MEALS

Recipes365

SOUTHERN PORK STEW

Those midday slumps can certainly put the rest of your day on a slippery slide. We're tired, we're getting hungry, and during the winter months the feeling to crawl under a blanket for a nap can be almost overwhelming. But fear not! We have the perfect dish that will put some warmth in your belly and a spring in your step. Ready? Well here we go.

SERVING SIZE:

You'll get 4 servings.

INGREDIENTS:

Spices:

1 tsp. oregano

1 tsp. paprika

¼ tsp. cinnamon

1 tsp. minced garlic

2 tsp. cumin

2. tsp. chilli powder

2 bay leaves

Salt and pepper to taste (approx ½ tsp. each)

Meat:

1 lb. cooked pork shoulder (sliced)

Vegetables:

½ green bell pepper (sliced)

½ red bell pepper (Sliced)

½ medium onion

6 oz. button mushrooms

½ jalapeno (sliced)

Soup:

¼ cup tomato paste

2 cups chicken broth

2 cups gelatinous bone broth

Juice: ½ lime

½ cup coffee (your remedy for the midday slump)

DIRECTIONS:

1. Clean and slice all your vegetables.

2. Add two tablespoons of Olive Oil to a pan and turn to high heat.

3. Sauté your vegetables until they are just beginning to cook and filling your kitchen with their fantastic aroma. Be careful not to overcook them here! That will give you a slightly mushy stew later on.

4. Set your slow cooker on low; add the bone broth, coffee, and chicken broth.

5. While your slow cooker is warming, add spices and bay leaves to a single bowl. This is a handy step for almost any recipe and will help you keep all your spices in one place.

6. Now add all your mushrooms and sliced pork to the slow cooker.

7. Give your cooking vegetables and oil a final stir, and add them to the crock pot along with all your spices.

8. Cover, and let the slow cooker work its magic for about 4-10 hours.

9. Once it's finished, remove the bay leaves (or keep an eye out for them), and serve!

And there you have it; a simple, hearty and unique dish to add a little sunshine to your lunchtime. Enjoy!

NUTRITIONAL INFORMATION (PER SERVING):

Calories: 386

Fat: 29g

Carbs: 6.5g

Protein: 19.8g

Keto Bacon Chicken Sandwich with Avocado

Sandwiches are no longer off limits on the keto diet! Make your bread using egg and cream cheese to keep the fat and protein content up, and top it with cheese and avocado!

SERVING SIZE:

The recipe yields 2 servings.

INGREDIENTS:

Bread:

1/4 tsp. salt

1/2 tsp. garlic powder

1/8 tsp. cream of tartar

3 large eggs

3 oz. cream cheese

Filling:

3 oz. chicken

2 slices bacon

2 slices pepper jack cheese

1 tsp. sriracha

1 tbsp. mayonnaise

2 grape tomatoes

1/4 avocado

DIRECTIONS:

1. Preheat oven to 300°F.

2. Separate your eggs into different bowls.

3. Add cream of tartar and salt to the eggs whites, and whip until you get soft peaks.

4. Add cream cheese to the egg yolks bowl and beat until a uniform pale yellow color forms.

5. Fold the egg white mixture into the yolks. Gently complete this as we want to the whites nice and airy.

6. Line a baking sheet with parchment paper, and pour about 1/4 cup of your bread mixture into individual areas, and form into square shapes.

7. Sprinkle garlic atop the bread and bake for 25 minutes.

8. While the bread is baking, cook the chicken and bacon with a little salt and pepper.

9. Once everything is cooked, assemble your sandwich with the mayo, avocado, cheese, and tomatoes.

Enjoy!

NUTRITIONAL INFORMATION (PER SERVING):

Calories: 355

Fat: 28g

Carbs: 1.5g

Protein: 24g

SPRING SALAD

Enjoy this light and sweet salad to keep you going for the afternoon. Bacon and pine nuts will help fill you up while the raspberry vinaigrette gives a distinctly sweet flavor.

SERVING SIZE:

This recipe yields 1 serving.

INGREDIENTS:

2 tbsp. parmesan (shaved)

2 tbsp. raspberry vinaigrette

2 oz. mixed greens

3 tbsp. pine nuts (roasted)

2 slices bacon

Salt and pepper to taste

DIRECTIONS:

1. Cook the bacon in a stovetop pan. Nice and crispy is what we're aiming for here!

2. Assemble your salad with the rest of the ingredients and crumble the bacon overtop.

3. Shake well to make sure everything in combined

Enjoy!

NUTRITIONAL INFORMATION (PER SERVING):

Calories: 470

Fat: 36g

Carbs: 4g

Protein: 17.5g

CHICKEN EGG SOUP

Easy and delicious lunchtime soup! Chicken broth and eggs yield a very savory dish while the extremely easy preparation makes it the perfect choice for a quick lunch.

SERVING SIZE:

This recipe yields 1 serving.

INGREDIENTS:

2 large eggs

1 tbsp. bacon fat

1 tsp. chili garlic paste

1/2 cube chicken bouillon

1 1/2 cups chicken broth

DIRECTIONS:

1. Heat a pan on medium-high, and add the broth, bacon fat, and bouillon cube.

2. Once the soup begins to boil, add the chili paste and stir continually for a minute. Now remove from heat.

3. Beat the eggs in a separate container, and pour into the broth.

4. Stir and let sit for about 30 seconds.

Serve and enjoy!

NUTRITIONAL INFORMATION (PER SERVING):

Calories: 275

Fat: 24g

Carbs: 2g

Protein: 13g

JALAPENO MUG CAKE

Missing out on lunch is a recipe for a disastrous afternoon. But even on the tightest of schedules, a quick mug cake can still get you a filling lunch! Here we have a zesty jalapeno mug cake made of egg and almond flour.

SERVING SIZE:

This recipe yields 1 serving.

INGREDIENTS:

1 large egg

1 tbsp. cream cheese

1 tbsp. butter

1 slice bacon

1/2 tsp. baking powder

1/2 jalapeno pepper

2 tbsp. almond flour

1 tbsp. golden flaxseed meal

1/4 tsp. salt

DIRECTIONS:

1. Heat a pan over medium, and cook the bacon until nice and crisp.

2. Now in a mug, mix all of the remaining ingredients. Scrape down the sides so everything is in the bottom of the mug.

3. Microwave for 80 seconds on high.

4. Flip the mug upside down and gently tap against a plate to make the cake fall out, and garnish with the bacon and any leftover jalapenos.

Enjoy!

NUTRITIONAL INFORMATION (PER SERVING):

Calories: 430

Fat: 36g

Carbs: 5g

Protein: 16g

ENCHILADA SOUP

This rich soup will certainly spice up your lunchtime! Chicken, cheese, and a little cayenne pepper will keep you running and on the keto diet at the same time.

SERVING SIZE:
The recipe yields 4 servings.

INGREDIENTS:
8 oz. cream cheese

4 cups chicken broth

6 oz. chicken (shredded)

4 stalks celery (diced)

1 red bell pepper (diced)

3 tbsp. olive oil

1/2 tsp. cayenne pepper

1/2 lime (juiced)

2 tsp. cumin

1 tsp. chili powder

1 tsp. oregano

2 tsp. garlic

1 cup tomatoes (diced)

1/2 cup cilantro (chopped)

DIRECTIONS:

1. Heat the olive oil in a pan on medium. Once hot, add the celery and pepper.

2. Once the celery is soft, toss in your tomatoes and cook until they begin to release their juice.

3. Add all your spices to the pan, and stir several times to incorporate.

4. Now add your cilantro and chicken broth to the pot, and crank up the heat to bring to a boil.

5. Once boiling, reduce heat to low, and simmer for 25 minutes.

6. Now add your cream cheese and again bring to a boil, then reduce heat, then simmer again for 30 minutes.

7. Add the shredded chicken to the pot as well as the lime juice. Stir several times to make sure everything is well mixed.

All set! Feel free to garnish with some cilantro or more cheese!

NUTRITIONAL INFORMATION (PER SERVING):

Calories: 350

Fat: 30g

Carbs: 5g

Protein: 14g

KETO PEPPER AND BASIL PIZZA

Lose the carb filled flour behind and swap in almond meal for the crust to this delicious lunchtime pizza. Keep it light with peppers and basil or pile on the meat, either way this is a keto friendly dish!

SERVING SIZE:

This recipe yields 2 servings (1/2 of one pizza).

INGREDIENTS:

Crust:

1 large egg

2 tbsp. cream cheese

2 tbsp. psyllium husk

1 tsp. Italian seasoning

2 tbsp. parmesan cheese

6 oz. mozzarella cheese

1/2 cup almond flour

1/2 tsp. each of salt and pepper

Toppings:

1/4 cup tomato sauce

3 tbsp. fresh basil (chopped)

4 oz. cheddar cheese (shredded)

2/3 bell pepper

1 vine tomato

DIRECTIONS:

1. Preheat your oven to 400°F.

2. Give your mozzarella (for the crust) a quick 45 second zap in the microwave to melt it.

3. Add all the other crust ingredients to the cheese and mix together completely.

4. Use your hands, or a rolling pin, to flatten the dough and make a circle.

5. Bake this for 10 minutes, and remove from the oven.

6. Now throw on all your toppings, and bake for an additional 10 minutes.

7. Remove pizza and let it cool

It's all yours!

NUTRITIONAL INFORMATION (PER SERVING):

Calories: 420

Fat: 30g

Carbs: 6g

Protein: 25g

Breezy Caprese Salad

Piles and piles of tomatoes, mozzarella and basil, what could be better? This simple lunch is delicious and filling, especially for those cheese hounds out there.

Serving size:

The recipe yields 2 servings.

Ingredients:

3 tbsp. olive oil

6 oz. mozzarella cheese

1 tomato

1/4 cup fresh basil (chopped)

Black pepper and salt to taste

DIRECTIONS:

1. Use a blender, or food processor, to pulse the basil and olive oil. This will leave you will a basil paste.

2. Now slice your tomato into about 1/4 "slices. We're looking for 6 slices here, so feel free to grab another tomato if you need to!

3. Cut the mozzarella into 1 oz. slices (right about the same size as the tomatoes or slightly thicker).

4. Layer your Caprese with the tomato as the base, then cheese, and topped with basil paste.

5. Season with salt and pepper to taste.

Dig in! Feel free to garnish with extra olive oil.

NUTRITIONAL INFORMATION (PER SERVING):

Calories: 406

Fat: 35g

Carbs: 5g

Protein: 17g

Keto Peanut Shrimp Curry

No need to stick to the hurried, unsatisfying, lunches we're used to. Give things a unique twist with this dish featuring shrimp and curry!

Serving Size:

This recipe yields 2 servings.

Ingredients:

1 tsp. fish sauce

1 tbsp. peanut butter

1 tsp. ginger (minced)

1 tsp. roasted garlic (crushed)

1 tbsp. soy sauce

1/4 tsp. xanthan gum

1/2 tsp. turmeric

3 tbsp. cilantro (chopped)

2 tbsp. coconut oil

1 spring onion (chopped)

1 cup vegetable stock

1/2 cup sour cream

1 cup coconut milk

5 oz. broccoli florets

2 tbsp. green curry paste

6 oz. shrimp (cooked)

1/2 lime (juiced)

DIRECTIONS:

1. Heat a pan over medium, and add the coconut oil. When hot, toss in the garlic, spring onion, and ginger.

2. Stir for a few minutes; and once cooked, add 1 tbsp. of the green curry paste. Along with your soy sauce, turmeric, peanut butter and fish sauce.

3. Continue to stir and cook for several minutes.

4. Now add the vegetable broth and coconut milk.

5. Add the xanthan gum, and mix completely.

6. When you notice the mixture begin to thicken, toss in the broccoli.

7. Continue to stir, and add the cilantro.

8. Lastly; add the shrimp and mix everything up. Allow it to cook for a few more minutes to allow the shrimp taste to develop.

Serve with your sour cream on top and enjoy!

NUTRITIONAL INFORMATION (PER SERVING):

Calories: 450

Fat: 32g

Carbs: 8.5g

Protein: 28g

CUCUMBER SALAD

Just like a mug cake, a salad can be the quick and easy solution to a hectic midday. Throw this cucumber salad together in mere minutes and enjoy the combination of noodles and cucumber.

SERVING SIZE:

This recipe yields 1 serving.

INGREDIENTS:

1/4 tsp. red pepper flakes

1 tbsp. rice vinegar

1 tbsp. sesame oil

1 tsp. sesame seeds

2 tbsp. olive oil

1 spring onion

1 packet shirataki noodles

3/4 large cucumber

salt and pepper to taste

DIRECTIONS:

1. Thoroughly rinse and wash your shirataki noodles, and allow them to dry on a paper towel.

2. Heat a pan over medium-high, and add the coconut oil.

3. Once the pan is hot, add your noodles and fry them for 6 minutes. They should shrink a great deal and any extra liquid will boil off.

4. Remove the noodles from the pan and again set them on a paper towel to dry.

5. Slice the cucumber into whatever sized slices you want, and arrange over a plate. Now top the cucumber with all the other ingredients (other than the noodles), and set in the fridge for 30 minutes.

6. Remove from the fridge, top with the noodles, and serve.

Enjoy!

NUTRITIONAL INFORMATION (PER SERVING):

Calories: 415

Fat: 44g

Carbs: 6g

Protein: 2g

PIZZAS ON PORTOBELLO

Don't want the carbs of ordinary pizza crust, but don't have the time to make your own? Then just throw down a couple Portobello mushrooms! These mushroom caps provide the perfect base to your midday pizza, and you can cook them to crispy or keep them soft, whichever you prefer!

SERVING SIZE:

This recipe yields 4 servings.

INGREDIENTS:

4 oz. mozzarella cheese

20 slices pepperoni

4 large Portobello mushroom caps

1 medium tomato

6 tbsp. olive oil

1/4 cup fresh basil (chopped)

salt and pepper to taste

DIRECTIONS:

1. Scrape the insides out from the mushroom caps. You want to just a have a shell here.

2. Coat the tops (not the insides) of the caps with your olive oil, and season with salt and pepper.

3. Broil the mushrooms for about 4 minutes, then flip and broil for an additional 3 to 4 minutes.

4. Slice your tomato into thin pieces, and place in the scooped out portion of the mushrooms.

5. Top the tomato with the basil

6. Now top the basil with the pepperoni slices and mozzarella cubes.

7. Broil for 3 to 4 minutes or until cheese starts to bubble.

All set to enjoy!

NUTRITIONAL INFORMATION (PER SERVING):

Calories: 320

Fat: 33g

Carbs: 2.5g

Protein: 8g

GINGER GLAZED SALMON

This savory ginger covered salmon is sure to put a smile on your face. A quick recipe with a savory combination of spices, this is sure to become a lunchtime favorite.

SERVING SIZE:

This recipe yields 2 servings.

INGREDIENTS:

1 tbsp. red boat fish sauce

2 tsp. garlic (minced)

1 tbsp. ketchup (sugar free)

1 tsp. ginger (minced)

1 tbsp. rice vinegar

2 tbsp. white wine

2 tbsp. soy sauce

2 tsp. sesame oil

10 oz. salmon fillet

DIRECTIONS:

1. Toss all of your ingredients except for the ketchup, white wine, and sesame oil into a container. Let these marinate for about 15 minutes.

2. Heat a pan on high and add the sesame oil.

3. As soon as the oil lets off a little smoke, add the fish with the skin side down.

4. Allow the fish skin to crisp up and cook, then flip and continue cooking. It generally takes about 3 to 4 minutes per side. After the first flip, add all the marinade ingredients to the pan and let them cook with the fish.

5. When cooked, remove the salmon from the pan. Add the ketchup and white wine to the liquid left in the pan.

6. Let everything simmer for 6 minutes, and put in side dish.

Serve it up with the sauce on the side.

NUTRITIONAL INFORMATION (PER SERVING):

Calories: 375

Fat: 22g

Carbs: 2g

Protein: 34g

EGG STUFFED AVOCADO

Turn the tables on the deviled egg! Instead of stuffing an egg, it's time to stuff an avocado with egg salad. Full of healthy fats and delicious spices, this easy recipe is a joy to prepare and eat.

SERVING SIZE:

This recipe yields 6 servings (each half of avocado is one serving).

INGREDIENTS:

2 tsp. brown mustard

1 tsp. hot sauce

4 tbsp. mayonnaise

2 tbsp. fresh lime juice

1/2 tsp. cumin

1/3 red onion

6 large eggs (hard boiled)

3 stalks celery

3 avocados

Salt and pepper to taste

DIRECTIONS:

1. Chop your onion, celery, and hard-boiled eggs.

2. In a bowl, combine all of the ingredients except the avocado.

3. Slice each avocado in half lengthwise and remove the pit.

4. Spoon your egg salad mixture into the center of each avocado slice.

Enjoy!

NUTRITIONAL INFORMATION (PER SERVING):

Calories: 300

Fat: 27g

Carbs: 4g

Protein: 8g

KETO TOMATO PESTO MUG CAKE

Another mug cake recipe for those hectic lunches! This tomato and pesto filled cake is tasty, and would make an excellent addition to some Caprese salad!

SERVING SIZE:
The recipe yields 1 serving.

INGREDIENTS:
2 tbsp. butter

2 tbsp. almond flour

1 large egg

1/2 tsp. baking powder

Pesto:

1 tbsp. almond flour

5 tsp. sun dried tomato pesto

1 pinch salt

DIRECTIONS:

1. Combine all ingredients in a mug (keep some pesto in reserve if you want it as a topping).

2. Microwave the mug on high for 70 to 80 seconds.

3. Light tap the mug against a plate and the mug will fall out.

4. Top with any leftover pesto

Quick and easy, enjoy!

NUTRITIONAL INFORMATION (PER SERVING):

Calories: 460

Fat: 45g

Carbs: 4g

Protein: 13g

KETO CABBAGE ROLLS WITH CORNED BEEF

These corned beef cabbage rolls are delicious, filling, and make a wonderful presentation if you're entertaining. The subtle hint of cloves and allspice provide an excellent finish to this dish!

SERVING SIZE:

This recipe yields 5 servings:

INGREDIENTS:

1 tbsp. erythritol

1 tbsp. bacon fat

1 fresh lemon

1 tbsp. brown mustard

1 tsp. whole peppercorns

2 tsp. Worcestershire sauce

1 tsp. mustard seeds

1/4 tsp. cloves

1/4 allspice

1/2 tsp. red pepper flakes

2 tsp. salt

1/4 cup coffee

1 medium onion

1/4 cup white wine

15 large cabbage leaves

1.5 lbs. corned beef

1 bay leaf (crushed)

DIRECTIONS:

1. In a slow cooker, combine all your spices, liquids, and the corned beef.

2. Turn the slow cooker to low, and leave for 6 hours.

3. When ready, bring a pot of water to boiling, and add all cabbage leaves as well as the sliced onion.

4. After 3 minutes remove the cabbage leaves, and dump them in some ice water for a further 4 minutes. Remember the onions should still be in the boiling water!

5. Slice the meat and dry off the cabbage leaves. Remove the onion from the water.

6. All the fillings into each cabbage leaf, and give a squirt of lemon juice overtop for good measure.

Enjoy!

NUTRITIONAL INFORMATION (PER SERVING):

Calories: 475

Fat: 27g

Carbs: 4g

Protein: 34.5g

KETO SAUSAGE PEPPER SOUP

This hearty soup is perfect for a drizzly lunchtime. It will leave your house, or office, with a wonderful aroma and the addition of hot sausage and jalapenos are sure to give you a kick!

SERVING SIZE:

This recipe yields 4 servings.

INGREDIENTS:

2 tsp. chili powder

2 tsp. garlic (minced)

2 tsp. cumin

1 tsp. Italian seasoning

1 green bell pepper

6 cups raw spinach

1/2 medium onion

1 can tomatoes with jalapenos

1.4 lbs. hot Italian sausage

2 cups beef stock

1/2 tsp. salt

1 red bell pepper

DIRECTIONS:

1. Tear the sausage into chunks and cook on the stove until fully cooked.

2. Slice your peppers; and add them, tomatoes, all spices, and beef stock to a crock pot.

3. Top the crock pot with the sausage and mix.

4. Fry your onions and garlic until the garlic begins to brown.

5. Add the onions and garlic to the crock pot, and top with the spinach.

6. Turn the crock pot to high, and cook for 3 hours.

7. After 3 hours, open it up and give everything a stir, then cook a further 2 hours.

Serve it up!

NUTRITIONAL INFORMATION (PER SERVING):

Calories: 380

Fat: 28g

Carbs: 7g

Protein: 25g

COCONUT CURRY

Would all the coconut lovers please stand up. We hope that includes most of you because this fantastic combination of curry and coconut is certain to give your lunch hour a zing!

SERVING SIZE:

This recipe yields 2 servings.

INGREDIENTS:

2 tsp. red boat fish sauce

1 tsp. garlic (minced)

2 tsp. soy sauce

1 tsp. ginger (minced)

1/2 cup coconut cream (or coconut milk)

4 tbsp. coconut oil

1 cup broccoli florets

1 tbsp. red curry paste

1/4 onion

1 large handful spinach

DIRECTIONS:

1. Add 2 tbsp. coconut oil to a pan on medium-high.

2. Chop your onion, and add it as well as the garlic to the pan.

3. When the garlic begins to brown, turn heat down to medium, and add broccoli.

4. Stir everything together, and when the broccoli is partially cooked, move everything to one side of the pan.

5. Add the curry paste to the open side of the pan, and let cook for 60 seconds.

6. Now toss the spinach on top of the broccoli until it begins to wilt, then add the coconut cream and rest of the oil.

7. Stir everything together, and add the fish sauce, ginger, and soy sauce. Let simmer for 10 minutes.

Enjoy!

NUTRITION INFORMATION (PER SERVING):

Calories: 395

Fat: 40g

Carbs: 7g

Protein: 6g

KETO TURKEY MEATBALLS

If it's a 'plate of meatballs all to myself' kind of day, or if you're in charge of appetizers for a party, these keto friendly turkey meatballs are just the ticket!

SERVING SIZE:

This recipe yields 20 servings/meatballs.

INGREDIENTS:

1/2 salt

1/2 pepper

3 sprigs thyme

2 large handfuls of spinach

3 small red chilies

10 slices bacon

2 lbs. ground turkey

1/2 green pepper

2 large eggs

1 oz. pork rinds

1 small onion

DIRECTIONS:

1. Line a baking sheet with foil, and place bacon on top. Preheat oven to 400°F.

2. Bake the bacon for 30 minutes, or until desired crispiness is reached.

3. While the bacon is cooking, add all ingredients (except ground turkey and spinach) to a food processor and mince well.

4. Add the minced mixture to the ground turkey and mix well.

5. Once the bacon is done, drain the fat into an individual container.

6. Now form 20 meatballs from your mixture and place on the same baking sheet that you used before.

7. Cook meatballs for 20 minutes or until the juice begins to run clear.

8. Skewer 2 to 3 pieces of bacon to each meatball.

9. Now in a food processor, blend the spinach, leftover bacon fat, and any spices you wish until you have a paste.

Serve the meatballs on top of the paste and enjoy!

NUTRITIONAL INFORMATION (PER SERVING):

Calories: 140

Fat: 10.5g

Carbs. 0.5g

Protein: 11g

PUMPKIN SOUP

A mellow soup bursting with autumn spice and pumpkin, this soup is perfect for fending off the cold as the seasons change. It's also an excellent remedy for a rainy day!

SERVING SIZE:

This recipe yields 3 servings (1 cup each).

INGREDIENTS:

1/2 tsp. pepper

1/2 tsp. salt

1/4 tsp. ginger (minced)

1/4 tsp. coriander

1/8 tsp. nutmeg

1/4 tsp. cinnamon

2 cloves garlic (roasted and minced)

4 tbsp. butter

1 cup pumpkin puree

1/2 cup heavy cream

4 slices bacon

1 bay leaf

1/4 onion (chopped)

3 tbsp. bacon grease

1 1/2 cups chicken broth

DIRECTIONS:

1. Add the butter to a sauce pan over medium-low heat, and heat until it begins to brown.

2. When the butter is dark golden in color, add your garlic, ginger, and onions

3. Cook for 3 minutes, and once the onions are translucent, add all of your spices and stir completely.

4. Cook for a further 2 minutes; then add the chicken broth and pumpkin.

5. Increase heat and bring to a boil. Once boiling, reduce heat and simmer for 20 minutes.

6. Transfer everything to a blender and puree until smooth or desired consistency.

7. Return to pot and simmer for a further 20 minutes.

8. Now cook your bacon in whatever style you wish.

9. When the soup is ready, add heavy cream and bacon grease. Mix well.

10. Crumble your bacon on top and serve.

Savor and enjoy!

NUTRITIONAL INFORMATION (PER SERVING):

Calories: 485

Fat: 47g

Carbs: 7.5g

Protein: 6g

CHICKEN SATAY

The upbeat combination of cayenne pepper, paprika, and peanut butter this a filling and enjoyable. Furthermore, we've kept the carb count down in order to keep you on your keto diet.

SERVING SIZE:

This recipe yields 3 servings.

INGREDIENTS:

1 tbsp. rice vinegar

2 tsp. chili paste

1/4 tsp. cayenne pepper

2 tsp. sesame oil

1 tbsp. erythritol

1 tsp. garlic (minced)

1/4 tsp. paprika

1/3 yellow pepper

4 tbsp. soy sauce

1 lb. ground chicken

2 spring onions

3 tbsp. peanut butter

1/2 lime (juiced)

DIRECTIONS:

1. Place pan on medium-high heat, and add sesame oil.

2. When hot, brown your chicken.

3. Add all other ingredients, except onion and yellow pepper, to the pan and mix well.

4. When everything is cooked all the way through, add your onion and pepper.

5. Continue to cook until onion is translucent.

6. Salt and pepper to taste and serve.

Nicely done, enjoy!

NUTRITIONAL INFORMATION (PER SERVING):

Calories: 390

Fat: 22g

Carbs: 3.5g

Protein: 34g

Bacon and Cheddar Mug Cake

The easy mug cake sure packs a punch! A hot bacon, cheddar, and chive cake that's delicious and only takes a few minutes!

SERVING SIZE:
This recipe yields 1 serving.

INGREDIENTS:
Base:

2 tbsp. almond flour

1 large egg

2 tbsp. butter

1/2 tsp. baking powder

Inner:

1 tbsp. white cheddar (shredded)

1 tbsp. chive (chopped)

1 tbsp. cheddar (shredded)

2 slices bacon

1/4 tsp. Mrs. Dash (table blend)

1 tbsp. almond flour

1 pinch salt

DIRECTIONS:

1. Mix all your base ingredients together. Stir well so there are no clumps.

2. Now chop your bacon (already cooked) and chives, and add these two along with all your innards ingredients together. Mix well.

3. Now mix everything together in a mug, and microwave on high for 70 seconds.

4. Lightly tap the mug against a plate and the cake will tumble out.

Serve it up! Add extra chives on top if you wish.

NUTRITIONAL INFORMATION (PER SERVING):

Calories: 570

Fat: 54g

Carbs: 6g

Protein: 25g

KETO INSIDE-OUT BURGER

Want to avoid the carbs in a burger? Then just toss 'em out! This inside out burger is absolutely delicious and features two patties forming the 'bun' stuffed with all your favorite burger toppings.

SERVING SIZE:

This Recipe yields 6 servings.

INGREDIENTS:

8 slices bacon (chopped)

2 tsp. garlic (minced)

28 oz. ground beef

2 tbsp. chives (chopped)

2 tsp. black pepper

1 tbsp. soy sauce

1 tsp. Worcestershire sauce

1 1/4 tsp. salt

1 tsp. onion powder

1/4 cup cheddar cheese

DIRECTIONS:

1. Heat up a cast iron skillet and cook your chopped bacon until nice and crispy. Remove to a paper towel once cooked and reserve the grease.

2. In a bowl, mix all of your spices, the ground beef, and 2/3 of the bacon. Mix completely.

3. Form about 9 patties.

4. Now toss about 2 tbsp. of the bacon fat back into the skillet.

5. Once hot and sizzling, add your patties and cook about 5 minutes.

6. Remove the patties from the pan and let them cool for about 5 minutes.

7. Serve them up with cheese, more bacon, and onion if you like. All your favorite burger toppings!

Enjoy!

NUTRITIONAL INFORMATION (PER SERVING):

Calories: 430

Fat: 35g

Carbs: 2g

Protein: 30g

SCRUMPTIOUS SUNDAY ROAST

Feeling ambitious for your weekend lunch? Then break out a beef rib roast and get it cooking in your slow cooker all morning, filling your house with a wonderful aroma in the process!

SERVING SIZE:

This recipe yields 8 servings.

INGREDIENTS:

1 tsp. garlic powder

2 tsp. salt

1 tsp. pepper

5 lbs. beef rib roast

DIRECTIONS:

1. Take your rib roast out of the fridge and let it come to room temperature for about an hour.

2. Pre heat your oven to 375°F.

3. Break out your roasting rack, or a casserole dish will work as well.

4. Give your roast a rub down with all your spices.

5. Place the roast in whatever oven safe dish you're using, and cook for 1 hour.

6. After 1 hour, turn off the oven, but **DO NOT** open the door. Let it sit in the turned off oven for another 3 hours. This will make your roast nice and tender.

7. About 45 minutes prior to serving, turn the oven back on to heat up the roast.

8. After removing from the oven, let the roast rest for about 15 minutes before slicing.

Serving with your favorite vegetables and enjoy!

NUTRITIONAL INFORMATION (PER SERVING):

Calories: 680

Fat: 45g

Carbs: 0.5g

Protein: 92g

CHICKEN STIR FRY WITH BACON

This quick stir fry features cheesy sausages amongst a pile of vegetables and swimming in a zesty sauce of pepper flakes and butter. Perfect for preparing on the weekend and taking to work throughout the week!

SERVING SIZE:

This recipe yields 3 servings.

INGREDIENTS:

2 tbsp. butter (salted)

1/2 tsp. pepper

2 tsp. garlic (minced)

1/2 tsp. red pepper flakes

1/2 cup parmesan cheese

3 cups broccoli florets

1/2 cup tomato sauce

3 cups spinach

1/4 cup red wine (merlot works well!)

1/2 tsp. salt

4 cheddar & bacon chicken sausages

DIRECTIONS:

1. Slice your sausage into whatever sizes you wish.

2. Heat a pan on high, and toss in your sausage. Also bring a separate pot of water to boiling.

3. Throw your broccoli into the boiling water. Cook for about 5 minutes or until it reaches your desired consistency.

4. Continue to stir your sausages as they cook, until they are uniformly brown.

5. Nudge your sausages to one side of the pan and then drop the butter onto the other side.

6. Drop your garlic into the butter and cook for 1 to 2 minutes.

7. Now stir everything in your pan together and add your broccoli as well.

8. Pour in the red wine and tomato sauce. Sprinkle the pepper flakes in as well.

9. Mix everything together. Add the spinach, salt, and pepper. Continue to stir as it cooks down.

10. Simmer for 10 minutes

You're all set, enjoy!

NUTRITIONAL INFORMATION (PER SERVING):

Calories: 450

Fat: 29g

Carbs: 8g

Protein: 36g

BEEFY STUFFED PEPPERS

The classic stuffed pepper with beef and bacon! Not a hassle to prepare and excellent for keeping in the fridge for future use.

SERVING SIZE:

This recipe yields 4 servings.

INGREDIENTS:

1 tsp. hot sauce

1 tbsp. garlic (minced)

1 tsp. liquid smoke

3 tbsp. olive oil

1 1/2 tsp. Worcestershire sauce

1 tbsp. soy sauce

2 tsp. oregano

1/2 tsp. black pepper

2 tbsp. ketchup (sugar free)

4 bell peppers

1 1/2 lbs. ground beef

4 slices bacon (thick cut)

DIRECTIONS:

1. Break out a Ziploc bag, and toss in your beef, spices, and oil. Seal the bag, and mix all the contents thoroughly.

2. Allow this bag to sit in the fridge for at least 3 hours.

3. Preheat your oven to 350°F, and bring a pot of salted water to a boil on the stove.

4. Blanch the peppers in the boiling water for 3 minutes, and then immediately remove and dry them.

5. Finely chop your bacon and give it a light fry, don't cook it all the way. Add this bacon to the beef mixture.

6. Now stuff the peppers with the bacon and beef mixture.

7. Bake the peppers for 55 minutes. If you have a meat thermometer, cook until the filling is at medium for beef.

8. Sprinkle some cheese on top, and broil until the cheese is bubbling.

Serve and enjoy!

NUTRITIONAL INFORMATION (PER SERVING):

Calories: 590

Fat: 42g

Carbs: 5g

Protein: 49g

CHEDDAR DRAPED MEATBALLS

What could make your classic meatballs even better? Wrap them in a cloak of cheddar cheese! These meatballs are prefect as the main event of your lunch, or an appetizer for a party.

SERVING SIZE:

This recipe yields 24 servings.

INGREDIENTS:

1 tsp. cumin

1 cup cheddar cheese

1 cup tomato sauce

1/3 pork rinds (crushed)

2 large eggs

1 tsp. chili powder

1 1/2 chorizo sausage

1 1/2 lbs. ground beef

1 tsp. salt

DIRECTIONS:

1. Preheat your oven to 350°F.

2. Break up your sausage and mix it with the ground beef. You want a fairly uniform mixture here.

3. Now add your pork rinds, spices, cheese, and eggs to the beef mixture. Combine well.

4. Form your meatballs and lay them on a foiled baking sheet.

5. Bake for about 35 minutes, or until fully cooked.

6. Drizzle the tomato sauce over the meatballs and serve.

Enjoy!

NUTRITIONAL INFORMATION (PER SERVING):

Calories: 113

Fat: 8g

Carbs: 1g

Protein: 10g

PEPPER JACK MEATBALLS

Another fantastic meatball recipe! Here we have pepper jack cheese, Italian sausage, and beef to keep the hunger at bay.

SERVING SIZE:

This recipe yields 11 servings / meatballs.

INGREDIENTS:

5 slices pepper jack cheese

1 tsp. oregano

2 large eggs

1/3 cup pork rinds (crushed)

1 cup alfredo sauce

1 tsp. Italian seasoning

1 1/2 hot Italian sausage.

1 1/2 lbs. ground beef

1 tsp. salt

DIRECTIONS:

1. Preheat your oven to 350°F.

2. Break up the sausage and mix with the beef.

3. Now add the eggs, pork rinds, and spices to the beef mixture. Mix well.

4. Grab about 2/3 of the meat you would need for each meatball and form into a semicircle.

5. Place the pepper jack cheese on top of the circle and then seal it up with the rest of the meat you need for that meatball.

6. Place the meatballs on a foiled baking sheet and bake for 40 minutes, or until completely cooked.

7. Drizzle with alfredo sauce and serve.

Enjoy!

NUTRITIONAL INFORMATION (PER SERVING):

Calories: 290

Fat: 20g

Carbs: 1.5g

Protein: 23g

CHEESE STUFFED HOTDOGS WITH BACON

Give your hotdogs some character by stuffing them with cheese! Better yet, wrap them in bacon for good measure!

SERVING SIZE:

This recipe yields 6 servings.

INGREDIENTS:

12 slices bacon

1/2 tsp. garlic powder

1/2 tsp. onion powder

2 oz. cheddar cheese

6 hotdogs

salt and pepper to taste

DIRECTIONS:

1. Preheat your oven to 400°F.

2. Slit all of the hotdogs lengthwise and stuff with the cheese.

3. Wrap the hotdogs with 2 slices of bacon each. Use toothpicks to secure the bacon.

4. Season to taste, and bake for 35 to 40 minutes.

Don't forget to take out the toothpicks, and enjoy!

NUTRITIONAL INFORMATION (PER SERVING):

Calories: 382

Fat: 35g

Carbs: 0.5g

Protein: 17g

BOK CHOY SALAD WITH TOFU

Here we have an interesting twist on the same old lunch salad. Switch things up by using bok choy, a thick leafy green, and cooking your own tofu. The tofu will have to be prepared the night before, but it's an excellent and filling lunch!

SERVING SIZE:
This recipe yields 3 servings.

INGREDIENTS:
Tofu:

1 tbsp. water

1 tbsp. soy sauce

2 tsp. garlic (minced)

1 tbsp. red wine vinegar

1 tbsp. sesame oil

15 oz. firm tofu

1/2 lemon (juiced)

Salad:

1 stalk green onion

2 tbsp. soy sauce

3 tbsp. coconut oil

1 tbsp. sambal olek

2 tbsp. cilantro (chopped)

9 oz. bok choy

1 tbsp. peanut butter

1/2 lime (juiced)

7 drops liquid stevia

DIRECTIONS:

1. Press dry the tofu. This will take nearly 6 hours.

2. Combine all of the tofu marinade ingredients and stir well.

3. Chop the tofu into uniform cubes, and drop into a plastics bag along with the marinade.

4. Let the tofu marinade overnight.

5. Now preheat your oven to 350°F.

6. Place the tofu on a backing sheet (on top of parchment paper), and bake for 35 minutes.

7. While this is baking, mix all the salad ingredients (except the choy). Add the cilantro and spring onion, and mix well.

8. Chop up the bok choy to whatever size you wish and remove the tofu from the oven.

Assemble your salad and enjoy!

NUTRITIONAL INFORMATION (PER SERVING):

Calories: 440

Fat: 36g

Carbs: 6g

Protein: 26g

KETO FRIENDLY NASI LEMAK

Take an adventure for your lunch and cook up some nasi lemak! This dish consists of rice and chicken cooked in coconut milk and is certain to give you some lunchtime flair!

SERVING SIZE:

This recipe yields 2 servings.

INGREDIENTS:

Chicken:

1/4 tsp. turmeric powder

1/8 tsp. salt

1/2 tsp. lime juice

1/2 tsp. curry powder

1/2 tsp. coconut oil

2 chicken thighs (boneless)

Nasi Lemak:

1/2 small shallot

1/4 tsp. salt

3 slices ginger

3 tbsp. coconut milk

7 oz. riced cauliflower

4 slices cucumber

Fried Egg:

1 large egg

1/2 tbsp. butter (unsalted)

DIRECTIONS:

1. Squeeze the water out of your riced cauliflower.

2. Combine your lime juice, salt, turmeric powder, and curry powder. Marinade the chicken thighs with this.

3. Fry the chicken until fully cooked.

4. Heat a saucepan, and toss in ginger, shallot, and coconut milk. Bring to a boil.

5. Once this is boiling, add the cauliflower rice and stir.

6. Fry your egg separately.

7. Dish up your rice mixture and eggs. Serve with 2 slices of cucumber.

All set!

NUTRITIONAL INFORMATION (PER SERVING):

Calories: 502

Fat: 40g

Carbs; 7g

Protein: 29g

"Food, in the end, in our own tradition, is something holy. It's not about nutrients and calories. It's about sharing. It's about honesty. It's about identity."

-Louise Fresco

KETOGENIC DIET

30 DELICIOUS DINNERS

1 MONTH OF LOW-CARB, HIGH-FAT WEIGHT LOSS MEALS

Recipes365

Nutty Salmon

This walnut crust salmon is sure to be a hit for dinner. Deliciously seasoned with mustard and dill, and it's packed with healthy fats to keep you on your diet.

Serving Size:
This recipe yields 2 servings.

Ingredients:
1/4 tsp. dill

1 tbsp. olive oil

1 tbsp. dijon mustard

2 salmon fillets (3 oz. each)

1/2 cup walnuts

2 tbsp. maple syrup (sugar free)

Salt and pepper to taste

DIRECTIONS:

1. Preheat your oven to 350°F.

2. Dump your syrup, mustard, and walnuts into a blender or food processor.

3. Pulse until you have a paste.

4. Heat a stovetop pan on high. Once hot, place your salmon skin side down in the pan.

5. Sear the salmon for about 3 minutes until the skin is crisp.

6. While searing the skin side, add the walnut paste to the side facing up.

7. Once done searing, transfer to the oven and bake for 7 to 8 minutes.

All done, enjoy!

NUTRITIONAL INFORMATION (PER SERVING):

Calories: 375

Fat: 44g

Carbs: 4g

Protein: 22g

CROCK POT OXTAILS

The crock pot is your best friend for dinner on a busy schedule. Just toss in the ingredients, forget for a few hours, and you've got a wonderful hot meal all ready. One such recipe is this crock pot oxtails dish.

SERVING SIZE:

This recipe yields 3 servings.

INGREDIENTS:

1 tsp. onion powder

3 tbsp. tomato paste

1 tsp. garlic (minced)

1 tbsp. fish sauce

2 tbsp. soy sauce

1 tsp. thyme (dried)

1/2 tsp. ginger (ground)

1/3 cup butter

2 lbs. oxtails

2 cups beef broth

1/2 tsp. guar gum

Salt and pepper to taste

DIRECTIONS:

1. Heat the beef broth on the stove, then add the fish sauce, tomato paste, soy sauce, and butter.

2. Once fully heated and mixed, add the mixture to a slow cooker and season with all your spices.

3. Add the oxtails to the slow cooker and mix well.

4. Set the slow cooker on low, and let cook for 7 hours.

5. Remove just the oxtails from the slow cooker, and set aside.

6. Now add the guar gum to what remains in the slow cooker, and use an immersion blender to pulse your mixture.

7. Now serve your oxtails and sauce along with your favorite side dish.

Enjoy!

NUTRITIONAL INFORMATION (PER SERVING):

Calories; 430

Fat: 30g

Carbs: 3.5g

Protein: 29g

KETO ASIAN STYLE SHORT RIBS

Give your standard ribs a delightful twist by throwing in some Asian style spice! The combination of ginger, soy sauce, and red pepper give this recipe a wonderful kick.

SERVING SIZE:

This recipe yields 4 servings.

INGREDIENTS:

Ribs and Marinade:

2 tbsp. rice vinegar

1/4 cup soy sauce

2 tbsp. fish sauce

6 large short ribs, flank cut (about 1.5 lbs.)

Asian Spice:

1/2 tsp. red pepper flakes

1/2 tsp. garlic (minced)

1/2 tsp. onion powder

1 tsp. ginger (ground)

1/2 tsp. sesame seed

1 tbsp. salt

1/4 tsp. cardamom

DIRECTIONS:

1. For the ribs, mix all of the marinade ingredients. Marinade the ribs for at least an hour.

2. Mix together all of the ingredients for the spice rub.

3. Remove the ribs from the marinade and rub with the spices from the previous step.

4. Heat your grill, and grill for approximately 5 minutes per side.

Bon appetite!

NUTRITIONAL INFORMATION (PER SERVING):

Calories: 415

Fat: 32g

Carbs: 1g

Protein: 30g

EASY PEEZY PIZZA

When you get home after a long day what can be better than a quick homemade pizza? With a crust of mostly egg and cheese, this keto pizza is delicious and customizable with all your favorite toppings!

SERVING SIZE:
This recipe yields 1 serving.

INGREDIENTS:
Crust:

1/2 tsp. Italian seasoning

1 tbsp. psyllium husk powder

2 large eggs

2 tsp. frying oil of choice

2 tbsp. parmesan cheese

Salt to taste

Toppings:

3 tbsp. tomato sauce

1 tbsp. basil (chopped)

1.5 oz. mozzarella cheese

DIRECTIONS:

1. Use a food processor, or blender, or immersion blender to combine all of the pizza crust ingredients.

2. Heat the oil in a frying pan, and add the crust mixture to the pan when hot. Spread into a circle.

3. Once the edges of the crust begin to brown, flip and cook for an additional 60 seconds.

4. Now top the crust with the cheese and tomato sauce, and broil for 2 minutes until the cheese begins to bubble.

Top with basil and enjoy!

NUTRITIONAL INFORMATION (PER SERVING):

Calories: 460

Fat: 36g

Carbs: 4g

Protein: 28g

SEARED RIBEYE

Ribeye, plain and simple. Just follow the recipe for searing and combine with your favorite fatty side dishes for a perfect keto friendly dinner!

SERVING SIZE:

This recipe yields 3 servings.

INGREDIENTS:

3 tbsp. bacon fat

salt and pepper to taste

2 medium ribeye steaks (about 1.25 lbs.)

DIRECTIONS:

1. Preheat your oven to 250°F.

2. Season the steaks with salt and pepper, then place on wire racks for baking.

3. Insert a meat thermometer into the streak.

4. Bake until the thermometer shows a temperature of 124°F.

5. Now heat a cast iron skillet on the stove and add your bacon grease. When very hot, sear your steaks for about 40 seconds per side.

All set, go eat!

NUTRITIONAL INFORMATION (PER SERVING):

Calories: 425

Fat: 32g

Carbs: 0g

Protein: 31g

KETO SALMON AND DILL SAUCE

The dill and salmon yields a delectable dish with the deep taste of salmon and a slight tangy hint of dill or sharp mustard. Give this salmon and dill sauce recipe a try and see for yourself!

SERVING SIZE:
This recipe yields 2 servings.

INGREDIENTS:
Salmon:

1 tbsp. duck fat

1 tsp. tarragon (dried)

1 tsp. dill weed (dried)

1 1/2 lbs. salmon fillet

Salt and pepper to taste.

Dill Sauce:

1/2 tsp. dill weed (dried)

1/4 cup heavy cream

1/2 tarragon (dried)

2 tbsp. butter

salt and pepper to taste

DIRECTIONS:

1. Slice your salmon so you have two fillets.

2. Season the meaty side with all of your salmon spices, and season the skin side with salt and pepper.

3. Heat a skillet over medium, and add the duck fat. When hot, add the salmon with the skin down.

4. Cook for about 5 minutes as the skin crisps. Once the skin is crispy, flip the salmon and reduce heat to low.

5. Cook for about 10 minutes, or until it is cooked to your liking.

6. When the salmon is removed from the pan, toss in all your spices for the dill sauce, and stir until they begin to turn brown.

7. Add the cream, and stir until hot.

Serve it up!

NUTRITIONAL INFORMATION (PER SERVING):

Calories: 465

Fat: 42g

Carbs: 2g

Protein: 23g

ORANGE DUCK BREAST

Give your duck some tang by mixing in some orange extract. A fun twist on the traditional duck roast, and sure to be an excellent dinner!

SERVING SIZE:

This recipe yields 1 serving.

INGREDIENTS:

1/2 tsp. orange extract

1 tbsp. swerve sweetener

1/4 tsp. sage

1 tbsp. heavy cream

2 tbsp. butter

1 cup spinach

6 oz. duck breast

DIRECTIONS:

1. Season the entire duck breast with salt and pepper, and score the top.

2. Heat a pan over medium-low, and add the butter and swerve. Cook until the butter begins to brown.

3. Add the orange extract and sage. Cook until the butter turns deep amber in color.

4. While this is cooking, set another pan on the stove and heat over medium-high. Add the duck breast to this pan.

5. Cook for a few minutes, or until the skin turns crisp. Then flip.

6. Now add the heavy cream to the butter mixture, and mix well.

7. When hot, pour the mixture over the duck breast, and cook for a further few minutes.

8. Toss the spinach into the pan and cook until wilted.

Enjoy!

NUTRITIONAL INFORMATION (PER SERVING)

Calories: 795

Fat: 72g

Carbs: 0g

Protein: 38g

CLASSIC RIBEYE

Steak, butter, and duck fat. That's all you need for this delicious ribeye along with some thyme for garnish. Try it with your favorite side dishes and enjoy!

SERVING SIZE:

This recipe yields 2 servings.

INGREDIENTS:

1 ribeye steak (~16 oz.)

1 tbsp. butter

1 tbsp. duck fat

1/2 tsp. thyme

Salt and pepper to taste

DIRECTIONS:

1. Preheat your oven to 400°F.

2. Place a cast iron skillet in the oven as it is warming.

3. Once the oven is up to temperature, remove the pan and place on the stove over medium heat.

4. Add the oil and steak to the pan. Sear the steak for about 2 minute

5. Turn over the steak, and bake in the oven for about 5 minutes.

6. Again remove the pan, and place over low heat on the stove.

7. Add your butter and thyme to the pan and mix with the oil.

8. Baste the steak for 4 minutes.

9. Let the steak rest for 5 minutes.

Put it into your face!

NUTRITIONAL INFORMATION (PER SERVING):

Calories: 748

Fat: 65g

Carbs: 0g

Protein: 39g

CHILI TURKEY LEGS

Give those turkey legs some spice by adding chili powder and cayenne pepper! This recipe is easy to follow and will provide you with a tasty and zippy end to your day.

SERVING SIZE:
This recipe yields 4 servings.

INGREDIENTS:
1/2 tsp. onion powder

1 tsp. liquid smoke

1/2 tsp. thyme (dried)

1/2 tsp. pepper

2 tsp. salt

1/4 tsp. cayenne pepper

1/2 tsp. garlic powder

1 tsp. Worcestershire sauce

1/2 tsp. ancho chili powder

2 turkey legs (about 1 lbs. each without bone)

2 tbsp. duck fat

DIRECTIONS:

1. Combine all dry spices in a bowl, then toss in the wet ingredients and mix thoroughly.

2. Dry the turkey legs with paper towel, and then rub in the seasoning.

3. Preheat oven to 350°F.

4. Heat a pan over medium-high, and add the duck fat.

5. When the oil begins to smoke, add the turkey legs and sear for 1 to 2 minutes per side.

6. Bake in the oven for 55 to 60 minutes or until completely cooked.

That's all folks!

NUTRITIONAL INFORMATION (PER SERVING):

Calories: 380

Fat: 21g

Carbs: 0.5g

Protein: 44g

SLOW ROASTED PORK SHOULDER

A hearty roasted pork shoulder to round off the day. Simple preparation, keto friendly, and excellent for entertaining!

SERVING SIZE:

This recipe yields 20 servings.

INGREDIENTS:

1 tsp. black pepper

2 tsp. oregano

1 tsp. onion powder

1 tsp. garlic powder

3 1/2 tsp. salt

8 lbs. pork shoulder

DIRECTIONS:

1. Preheat oven to 250°F.

2. Dry the pork, then rub with the salt and spices.

3. Place the shoulder on a wire rack (a foiled baking sheet works too), and bake for 8 to 10 hours. Or until your meat thermometer reads 190°F.

4. Remove from the oven, and raise oven temperature to 500°F.

5. Cover the shoulder with foil and let rest for about 15 minutes.

6. Remove the foil from the shoulder, and roast in the oven for another 20 minutes, while rotating every 5 minutes.

7. Remove from oven and let rest for 20 minutes.

Serve this bad boy up!

Nutritional information (per serving):

Calories: 460

Fat: 35g

Carbs: 0.5g

Protein: 32g

Asian Spiced Chicken Thighs

Liven up your chicken thighs with some sriracha and red pepper! These zippy little devils provide an excellent laid-back dinner, or a quick snack during the day!

SERVING SIZE:

This recipe yields 4 servings.

INGREDIENTS:

1 tsp. ginger (minced)

1 tsp. garlic (minced)

1/4 tsp. xanthan gum

1 tsp. red pepper flakes

1 tbsp. ketchup (sugar free)

1 tbsp. olive oil

1 tbsp. rice wine vinegar

2 tsp. sriracha

4 cups spinach

6 chicken thighs (bone in and skin on)

Salt and pepper to taste

DIRECTIONS:

1. Preheat your oven to 425°F.

2. Dry your chicken and season the skin with salt and pepper.

3. Mix all of the sauce ingredients until a paste begins to form

4. Rub this sauce all over the chicken.

5. Lay the chicken on a wire rack

6. Bake for 45 to 50 minutes, or until the skin is crisp and slight charring appears.

7. Mix the spinach, some salt and pepper, red pepper flakes, and leftover chicken fat together, and serve alongside the baked chicken.

Enjoy!

NUTRITIONAL INFORMATION (PER SERVING):

Calories: 600

Fat: 52g

Carbs: 2g

Protein: 30g

BAKED POBLANO PEPPERS

Very similar to baked stuffed mushrooms, these peppers combine pork, mushrooms, cumin, and chili powder for a delicious dinner!

SERVING SIZE:

This recipe yields 4 servings.

INGREDIENTS:

7 baby bella mushrooms

1/2 onion

1/4 cup cilantro

4 poblano peppers

1 tsp. chili powder

1 tsp. cumin

1 tomato

1 tbsp. bacon fat

1 lb. ground pork

Salt and pepper to taste

DIRECTIONS:

1. Broil your poblano peppers in the oven for about 10 minutes. Flip or move every couple minutes to keep broiling consistent.

2. Heat a pan on the stove, and add the bacon fat. Once browned, add the cumin, chili, salt, and pepper.

3. Dice the onion and toss into the mixture, along with the garlic. Fully mix, and then add the mushrooms

4. Once the mushrooms are cooked, add the cilantro and chopped tomato.

5. Cook for a further 3 minutes.

6. Stuff the poblanos with the mixture and bake at 350°F for 9 to 10 minutes.

You're all done!

NUTRITIONAL INFORMATION (PER SERVING):

Calories: 365

Fat: 28g

Carbs: 6g

Protein: 22g

Coconut Shrimp

Shrimp with a tropical flair! Coconut crusted with a fruity apricot sauce, this keto recipe will fill you up for dinner and also keep those sweet cravings in check.

SERVING SIZE:

This recipe yields 3 servings.

INGREDIENTS:

Shrimp:

1 cup coconut flakes (unsweetened)

2 large egg whites

1 lb. shrimp (peeled and deveined)

2 tbsp. coconut flour

Sauce:

1 tbsp. lime juice

1 1/2 tbsp. rive wine vinegar

1 medium red chili (diced)

1/2 apricot preserves (sugar free)

1/4 tsp. red pepper flakes

DIRECTIONS:

1. Preheat your oven to 400°F

2. Beat the egg whites until soft peaks form.

3. Dip the shrimp in the coconut flour, then dip in the egg whites, then dip in the coconut flakes.

4. Lay the dipped shrimp on a greased baking sheet.

5. Bake the shrimp for 15 minutes

6. Finish them off with a 3 to 5 minute broil to give them some browning.

7. Combine all of the ingredients for the sauce and mix well.

Serve them up and enjoy!

NUTRITIONAL INFORMATION (PER SERVING):

Calories: 395

Fat: 22g

Carbs: 7g

Protein: 37g

Slow Cooked Lamb

Break out that slow cooker for this fantastic leg of lamb stuffed with savory herbs. Get it prepared in just a few minutes and let the cooker do the rest!

Serving size:

This recipe yields 6 servings

Ingredients:

3/4 tsp. rosemary (dried)

6 leaves mint

1 tbsp. maple syrup

2 tbsp. whole grain mustard

3/4 tsp. garlic

1/4 cup olive oil

2 lbs. leg of lamb

Salt and pepper to taste

4 sprigs thyme

DIRECTIONS:

1. Cut three slits across the top of the lamb.

2. Heat a slow cooker to low, and rub the lamb with olive oil, syrup, mustard, salt, and pepper.

3. Stuff each slit on the lamb with garlic and rosemary

4. Add to the slow cooker and leave for 7 hours.

5. Add thyme and mint to slow cooker and leave for an additional hour.

Enjoy!

NUTRITIONAL INFORMATION (PER SERVING):

Calories: 415

Fat: 35g

Carbs: 0.5g

Protein: 27g

CHICKEN WITH PAPRIKA

This keto chicken recipe combines sweet and spicy in the form of maple syrup and paprika. Cook this savory chicken in its sauce then drizzle right before serving.

SERVING SIZE:
This recipe yields 4 servings.

INGREDIENTS:
2 tbsp. Spanish smoked paprika

3 tbsp. olive oil

1 tbsp. maple syrup

2 tbsp. lemon juice

2 tsp. garlic (minced)

4 chicken breasts (boneless and skinless)

Salt and pepper to taste

DIRECTIONS:

1. Preheat your oven to 350°F.

2. Cut the chicken into chunks and season with the salt and pepper.

3. Combine all other ingredients separately to make the sauce.

4. Add about 1/3 of the sauce to your baking casserole dish or pan. Lay chicken on top of sauce.

5. Drizzle the rest of the sauce over the chicken.

6. Bake for 30 to 35 minutes, and then broil for a further 5 minutes.

Serve!

NUTRITIONAL INFORMATION (PER SERVING):

Calories: 275

Fat: 13.5g

Carbs: 2.5g

Protein: 36.5g

Curried Chicken Thighs

A straight forward, keto friendly method for whipping up some curried chicken. Easy to cook and excellent for those tired weeknights!

Serving Size:

This recipe yields 8 servings.

Ingredients:

1/2 tsp. chili powder

1/2 tsp. coriander (ground)

1/2 tsp. cinnamon (ground)

1/2 tsp. cayenne pepper

1/2 tsp. allspice

1/2 tsp. cardamom (ground)

1/4 tsp. ginger

1 tsp. cumin (ground)

1 tsp. paprika

1 tsp. garlic powder

2 tsp. yellow curry

8 chicken thighs (bone in and skin on)

1/4 cup olive oil

1 1/2 tsp. salt

DIRECTIONS:

1. Preheat oven to 425°F.

2. In a bowl, mix all of your spices together.

3. Line a baking sheet with foil, and place all the chicken on the foil.

4. Rub the olive oil and spices over the chicken.

5. Bake for 50 minutes are until completely cooked.

6. Cool for 5 to 8 minutes.

Go enjoy your evening!

NUTRITIONAL INFORMATION (PER SERVING):

Calories: 278

Fat: 20g

Carbs: 0.5g

Protein: 22g

APPLEWOOD PORK CHOPS

Give your pork chops a subtle hint of Applewood and delicious dinner is all yours! Combine with your favorite fatty side dish and you've an excellent keto meal right in front of you.

SERVING SIZE:

This recipe yields 4 servings.

INGREDIENTS:

1/2 tsp. garlic powder

1 tsp. grill mates Applewood rub

1/2 tsp. black pepper

1/2 tsp. Mrs. Dash (table blend)

1 tsp. salt

2 tbsp. olive oil

2 2tsp. hidden valley powdered ranch

4 pork chops (bone in)

DIRECTIONS:

1. Combine all of the spices and rub into the pork chops.

2. Heat a pan on medium, and add the olive oil.

3. When hot, add the pork chops and cover.

4. Cook for about 10 minutes and then flip the chops.

5. Cook for a further 5 minutes (covered).

6. Turn the heat up to high, and flip chops again. Keep the pan uncovered now.

7. Cook for 2 minutes, and then let rest for 4 minutes

Serve and enjoy!

NUTRITIONAL INFORMATION (PER SERVING):

Calories: 260

Fat: 13g

Carbs: 1.5g

Protein: 35g

CHICKEN STEW

Whether it's a chilly, rainy, or stormy day; good old fashioned chicken stew is an excellent choice for dinner. Warming and comforting, this recipe fits the bill with some extra zip from hot wing sauce.

SERVING SIZE:
This recipe yields 5 servings.

INGREDIENTS:
2 tsp. garlic (minced)

3 tbsp. butter

2 tsp. paprika

2 tsp. ranch seasoning

1 tsp. red pepper flakes

1 tsp. oregano

1/2 cup sliced tomatoes

1 1/2 tomato sauce

3 lbs. chicken thigh

1 green pepper

1/3 cup hot wing sauce

3 cups mushrooms

DIRECTIONS:

1. Finely slice your mushrooms and pepper.

2. Set your crock pot on high and add the thighs, tomato slices, garlic, spices, tomato sauce, and hot sauce.

3. Also toss in peppers and mix.

4. Let the mixture cook for 2 hours.

5. Now turn the pot to low, give the mix a stir, and cook for 4 to 5 hours.

6. Dump in 3 tbsp. of butter and give another stir.

7. Remove the lid, and cook for an hour.

Savor the glory!

NUTRITIONAL INFORMATION (PER SERVING):

Calories: 360

Fat: 22g

Carbs: 8g

Protein: 33g

ASIAN PORK CHOPS

Once again, give the 'old reliable' recipes an upgrade by including some Asian style spices. Here we have pork chops mixed with anise, soy sauce, and sesame oil to create a unique and enjoyable culinary experience.

SERVING SIZE:

This recipe yields 2 servings.

INGREDIENTS:

1/2 tbsp. sambal chili paste

1/2 tsp. five spice

1/2 tbsp. ketchup (sugar free)

1 stalk lemon grass

4 garlic cloves (halved)

1 tbsp. almond flour

1 tbsp. fish sauce

1/2 tsp. peppercorns

1 1/2 tsp. soy sauce

1 tsp. sesame oil

1 medium star anise

4 boneless pork chops

DIRECTIONS:

1. Pound the pork chops to 1/2 inch thickness

2. Grind the peppercorns and star anise to a fine powder.

3. Combine the pepper, anise, lemongrass, and garlic. Grind until a paste forms.

4. Marinade the chops with the paste

5. Let the chops marinate for about 2 hours at room temperature.

6. Heat a pan on high. Coat your pork chops with the almond flour.

7. Sear the chops in the pan. This should take about 1 to 2 minutes per side.

8. Once the pork is cooked, cut them into slices.

9. Mix the sambal and ketchup to create your sauce.

Enjoy your masterpiece!

NUTRITIONAL INFORMATION (PER SERVING):

Calories: 275

Fat: 10g

Carbs: 5g

Protein: 35g

PORTOBELLO BURGERS

The constant battle to avoid the carbs in bread can be draining. But you can still have a good old fashioned burger! Dive into this recipe with the twist of mushrooms for the buns.

SERVING SIZE:
This recipe yields 1 serving.

INGREDIENTS:
Bun:

1 tsp. oregano

1 clove garlic

1/2 tbsp. coconut oil

2 Portobello mushroom caps

1 pinch each of salt and pepper

Burger:

1 tsp. each of salt and pepper

6 oz. beef

1 tbsp. dijon mustard

1/4 cup cheddar cheese

DIRECTIONS:

1. Preheat a griddle on high

2. In a container, combine the oil and spices for the bun

3. Scrape out the insides of the mushrooms, and marinate in the oil and spices

4. In a separate bowl, combine the meat, salt, pepper, cheese, and mustard.

5. Use your hands to form your burger patties.

6. Now add your mushrooms to the griddle and cook about 8 minutes.

7. Remove the mushrooms and toss the patties on. Cook about 5 minutes per side.

8. Assemble your burger with whatever toppings you like.

That's it!

NUTRITIONAL INFORMATION (PER SERVING):

Calories: 730

Fat: 46g

Carbs: 5g

Protein: 62g

BBQ Chicken Pizza

Slash the carbs in your pizza by making your own crust out of eggs and cheese! This recipe for BBQ chicken pizza will guide you through the quick and painless process of making your own pizza crust, along with some delectable toppings.

Serving Size:

This recipe yields 4 servings.

Ingredients:

Crust:

1 1/2 tsp. Italian seasoning

6 tbsp. parmesan cheese

3 tbsp. psyllium husk powder

6 large eggs

salt and pepper to taste

Toppings:

1 tbsp. mayonnaise

4 tbsp. tomato sauce

6 oz. rotisserie chicken (shredded)

4 tbsp. BBQ sauce

4 oz. cheddar cheese

DIRECTIONS:

1. Pre heat your oven to 425°F.

2. Combine all ingredients for the crust in a blender and pulse until thick. An immersion blender will serve this purpose as well.

3. Now spread the dough into a circle on a baking sheet or oven stone. Be sure you grease the surface first.

4. Bake for 10 minutes.

5. Flip the crust over, and pile up your toppings.

6. Broil for a further 10 minutes.

Enjoy, you deserve it.

NUTRITIONAL INFORMATION (PER SERVING):

Calories: 355

Fat: 25g

Carbs: 3g

Protein: 25g

CHEESE STUFFED BURGER

Imagine taking a bit from a juicy burger, and suddenly, there's cheese! The cheese stuffed burger, or the Juicy Lucy, is sure to be a grill or dinnertime favorite.

SERVING SIZE:

This recipe yields 2 servings / burgers.

INGREDIENTS:

1 oz. mozzarella cheese

1/2 tsp. pepper

1 tsp salt

2 oz. cheddar cheese

1 tsp. Cajun seasoning

1 tbsp. butter

2 slices bacon (cooked)

8 oz. ground beef

DIRECTIONS:

1. Use your hands to work all the spices into the beef.

2. Form your patties with the mozzarella cheese stuffed inside

3. Heat a pan on the stove and add 1 tbsp. of butter. When hot, add burger to the pan and cover.

4. Cook 2 to 3 minutes, flip, and sprinkle cheese on top. Cover again and cook to taste.

5. Feel fresh to recharge the butter in between burgers if you wish.

6. Chop your bacon and top the burgers.

Voila, ready to go!

NUTRITIONAL INFORMATION (PER SERVING):

Calories: 612

Fat: 50g

Carbs: 2g

Protein: 32g

TATER TOT STYLE NACHOS

What happens when you combine two cheesy side dishes? You get one amazingly delicious dinner course! This recipe for tater tot nachos tastes just as good as it sounds.

SERVING SIZE:
This recipe yields 2 servings.

INGREDIENTS:
6 oz. ground beef (cooked)

2 tbsp. sour cream

6 black olives

1 tbsp. salsa

1/2 jalapeno (sliced)

2 oz. cheddar cheese

2 tater tots (preferably homemade)

DIRECTIONS:

1. In a small cast iron skillet (or casserole dish) place 10 tots as the base layer.

2. Now add half of your beef and cheddar cheese. Repeat this stack-up again until you use all your ingredients.

3. Broil the dish for about 5 minutes until the cheese is fully melted and bubbly.

4. Serve with the black olives, sour cream, and jalapenos.

Enjoy!

NUTRITIONAL INFORMATION (PER SERVING):

Calories: 635

Fat: 53g

Carbs: 6g

Protein: 30g

CHIPOTLE CHICKEN WINGS WITH BLACKBERRY JAM

Game day for your favorite team? Have to bring food to a get together? Then whip up these tasty chipotle style chicken wings! Great for sharing or keep them all to yourself, and the blackberry jam in the next recipe makes the perfect side.

SERVING SIZE:

This recipe yields 5 servings

INGREDIENTS:

1/2 cup chipotle jam with blackberries (see next recipe)

1/2 cup water

3 lbs. chicken wings (~20)

Salt and pepper to taste

DIRECTIONS:

1. Combine the jam and water in a bowl using a fork or whisk to make sure everything is well mixed.

2. In a plastic bag, add all of the chicken, about 2/3s of the jam, salt, and pepper to taste. Make sure everything is well combined and leave to marinate for at least an hour.

3. Preheat oven to 400°F.

4. Lay the chicken on a greased baking sheet, and back for 15 minutes.

5. Flip the chicken, crank the temperature to 425°F, spread the remaining sauce over top, and back for another 25 to 30 minutes.

Eat as is or add the next recipe in.

NUTRITIONAL INFORMATION (PER SERVING):

Calories: 500

Fat: 40g

Carbs: 1.5g

Protein: 35g

CHIPOTLE JAM WITH BLACKBERRY

The spicy and fruity combination in this chipotle style blackberry jam makes this sauce an excellent accompaniment for almost any meat. We recommend dishing it up with our recipe for chipotle chicken wings.

SERVING SIZE:

This recipe yields 10 servings / tablespoons.

INGREDIENTS:

8 drops liquid stevia

1/4 cup MCT oil

1/4 cup erythritol

1/4 tsp. guar gum

8 oz. blackberries

1 1/2 whole chipotle peppers

DIRECTIONS:

1. Heat a pan over low, and add the blackberries. Cook until they are soft and have released their juices.

2. Add everything except the oil and guar gum to the pan. Use a fork to crush the blackberries and mix well.

3. Now turn up the heat to medium, add the oil, and bring to a boil.

4. Once boiling, reduce heat and simmer for a good 8 minutes.

5. Add the guar gum, and mix completely. Using a colander, strain the mixture into a container.

Stick on the side of a dish or eat solo!

NUTRITIONAL INFORMATION (PER SERVING):

Calories: 50

Fat: 6g

Carbs: 1.5g

Protein: 0.5g

JALAPENO SOUP

If you're ready to take a break from the standard savory soups and stews, then give this jalapeno soup a try! Creamy and full of chicken this recipe will satisfy your spicy side (especially if you keep the jalapeno seeds in!)

SERVING SIZE:

This recipe yields 6 servings.

INGREDIENTS:

1 tsp. cilantro (dried)

1 tsp. onion powder

1 tsp. Cajun seasoning

1 tbsp. chicken fat

3 jalapenos (diced)

3 cups chicken broth

4 slices bacon (cooked)

6 oz. cream cheese

4 oz. cheddar cheese

4 chicken thighs (deboned)

salt and pepper to taste

2 tsp. garlic (minced)

DIRECTIONS:

1. Preheat your oven to 400°F.

2. Rub the seasoning onto the chicken and bake for 50 to 55 minutes.

3. Heat a pan over medium-high and add the chicken fat. Once hot, add your chicken bones and fry them for 10 minute.

4. Toss in the garlic and jalapenos. Stir and cook for another 4 minutes.

5. Now pour in the broth and spices. Continue to simmer while the chicken bakes.

6. Remove the chicken skin from the thighs and the bones from the pot.

7. Use an immersion blender to puree the jalapenos and garlic. Shred the meat and add to the pot.

8. Simmer for a further 10 minutes

9. Add the cream cheese and cheddar cheese. Stir to fully incorporate and simmer for 10 more minutes.

Garnish with the bacon and enjoy!

NUTRITIONAL INFORMATION (PER SERVING):

Calories: 550

Fat: 43g

Carbs: 4g

Protein: 34g

Bacon Cheddar Soup

When is it not a good time for bacon and cheese? Yup, that's what we thought. So dive into this bacon cheddar soup with gusto and enjoy!

Serving size:

This recipe yields 5 servings.

Ingredients:

1 tsp. garlic powder

1/2 tsp. celery seed

1 tsp. thyme (dried)

1 tsp. onion powder

3/4 cup heavy cream

1/2 tsp. cumin

3 cups chicken broth

4 tbsp. butter

1/2 lbs. bacon

8 oz. cheddar cheese

Salt and pepper to taste

4 jalapeno peppers (diced)

DIRECTIONS:

1. Chop up the bacon to 1 inch slices. Cook until crisp and save the fat.

2. Now dice your jalapenos and cook in the saved bacon fat.

3. Now toss the bacon fat (we're still using it!) into a pot, along with the butter, spices, and broth. Bring the pot to a boil.

4. Once boiling, reduce heat and simmer for 15 minutes.

5. Use a food processor or immersion blender to puree the mixture. Then add the cream and shredded cheese.

6. Stir everything together and keep simmering. Salt and pepper to taste.

7. Add jalapenos and bacon to the pot and simmer for a final 5 minutes.

Enjoy!

NUTRITIONAL INFORMATION (PER SERVING):

Calories: 520

Fat: 50g

Carbs: 4g

Protein: 20g

Keto Chicken Nuggets

Have a hankering for some fast food chicken nuggets? Then make your own keto version! This recipe will satisfy your craving while still keeping you firmly on the ketogenic diet.

SERVING SIZE:

This recipe yields 4 servings.

INGREDIENTS:

Nuggets:

1/4 tsp. paprika

1/4 tsp. salt

1/4 tsp pepper

1/8 tsp. onion powder

1/8 tsp. cayenne pepper

1/4 tsp. chili powder

1/8 tsp. garlic powder

zest from 1 lime

1/4 cup almond flour

1 large egg

24 oz. chicken thighs

1.5 oz. pork rinds

1/4 cup flax meal

Sauce:

1 tbsp. lime juice

1/8 tsp. cumin

1/4 tsp. garlic powder

1/2 tsp. red chili flakes

1/2 avocado

1/2 cup mayonnaise

DIRECTIONS:

1. Add all the ingredients for the crust to a food processor and pulse together.

2. Put the crumbs in a bowl.

3. Whisk the egg is in separate container.

4. Dip each piece of chicken in the eggs and then crumbles, and lay on a greased baking tray.

5. Heat the oven to 400°F, and back for 15 to 18 minutes.

6. Make the sauce by combining all of the sauce ingredients, and mixing well.

Feast!

NUTRITIONAL INFORMATION (PER SERVING):

Calories: 612

Fat: 49g

Carbs: 2g

Protein: 39g

PORK TACOS

Here's your keto version of the classic pork taco. Pepper, lettuce, and pork and flax seed tortillas; easy to put together and add any other toppings that you feel like!

SERVING SIZE:
This recipe yields 3 servings.

INGREDIENTS:
1/4 tsp. garlic powder

1/4 tsp. oregano

3/4 yellow pepper

1/4 tsp. onion powder

1 lbs. pork shoulder (cooked)

1 tbsp. olive oil

1/2 tsp. salt

1/2 tsp. chipotle powder

1 jalapeno pepper

1 cup romaine lettuce

6 thin flax tortillas

1/4 tsp. pepper

DIRECTIONS:

1. Chop your pork into cubes. You can also shred it if you wish.

2. Combine all spices and oil, and add to plastic bag.

3. Toss the pork into the plastic bag and marinade for at least 45 minutes.

4. Heat 1 tbsp. olive oil in a sauce pan set to high heat; chop the vegetables and add to pan.

5. When vegetables are done, cook the pork on high heat until completely done and crisp.

6. Assemble your tacos with the vegetables, lettuce, and pork

Enjoy!

NUTRITIONAL INFORMATION (PER SERVING):

Calories: 715

Fat: 68g

Carbs: 3.5g

Protein: 36g

CHICKEN DRESSED AS BACON

This chicken can't pull the wool over our eyes; even though it will look like one giant slab of bacon once you wrap your bacon slices around the outside, and then bake it in a remarkable lemon mustard sauce. Sounds good doesn't it?

SERVING SIZE:

This recipe yields 8 servings.

INGREDIENTS:

1 small lime

1 tbsp. grain mustard

1 medium lemon

10 strips bacon

3 lbs. whole chicken (gutted)

4 sprigs fresh thyme

Salt and pepper to taste

DIRECTIONS:

1. Preheat oven to 500°F.

2. Season the chicken with salt and pepper, and stuff with the lemon, lime, and thyme.

3. Season bacon with salt and pepper and wrap over the chicken any way you wish.

4. Add the chicken to a roasting pan, and bake for 15 minutes.

5. Lower temperature to 350°F, and bake for a further 45 minutes.

6. Take the chicken out of the pan and place in foil, and transfer the fat and juice to a stovetop pan.

7. Bring pan to a boil and add mustard. Mix well.

Serve with the sauce on the side!

NUTRITIONAL INFORMATION (PER SERVING):

Calories: 375

Fat: 30g

Carbs: 2g

Protein: 24g

"I like food. I like eating. And I don't want to deprive myself of good food."

-Sarah Michelle Gellar

FREE BONUS GUIDE:
TOP 10 KETO DIET MISTAKES

We hope you enjoy making your way through the delicious meals contained in this cookbook.

To ensure you stay safe and maximize your progress be sure to pick up your free bonus guide below now to avoid the top 10 keto diet mistakes!

Visit www.litomedia.com/ketogenic-mistakes to get your free bonus guide!

LIKE THIS BOOK?

If you enjoyed the meals in this cookbook, please visit your Amazon order history to leave a review and let us know.

If you also downloaded the free bonus guide, you will know the value of community, so don't forget to share this book with a friend too!

Made in the USA
Middletown, DE
03 February 2017